San Diego

Irving Weisdorf & Co. Ltd.

INTRODUCTION

Picture the perfect destination: It is a sunny place with clear blue skies and a warm climate freshened by cool coastal breezes. It is a vibrant metropolis without an attitude, but with the easy-going nature of a people who get a lot done without seeming to be in a hurry. It is a community with a proud heritage that blends its modern architecture with old-town history. It is a place of gently swaying palms, sandy beaches, cool canyons and intriguing desert and mountain terrain, all within easy reach. Picture this perfect destination. It is a city called **San Diego.**

Situated in the southwestern-most corner of California, America's sixth-largest city is actually a collection of diverse communities spread across San Diego County, an area the size of the state of Connecticut. The communities of San Diego are composed - in large part - of native Californians, Mexican immigrants, military personnel, and retirees from all over the United States. Once little more than a semi-transparent resort town with a Mexican flavor, San Diego now boasts more than 2.6-million residents and a varied economy based in agriculture, manufacturing, aerospace technology, electronics, aircraft and ship-building, scientific research and especially, tourism. Many resident San Diegans came here first as tourists, tourists who agree that the perfect destination is also the perfect place to call home.

The palms and towers of San Diego's downtown.

Downtown as seen from the San Diego-Coronado Island ferry landing.

A lonely, lovely stretch of beach at sundown.

POINT LOMA

A Portuguese explorer sailing under the flag of Spain gets the credit for discovering the rocky shores and sandy beaches of what was then just an arid land of scrub brush and dusty hills. But **Juan Rodriguez Cabrillo** was taken by the natural harbor and the surrounding beauty of the area, so his two wooden ships landed at **Point Loma** on September 28, 1542. Cabrillo probably climbed a nearby rocky promontory, picking his way through the sage and cacti - just as visitors do today - to get a better view of the area he called San Miguel. Today Cabrillo's rugged statue stands atop that promontory, a striking figure against a breathtaking view of San Diego and the snow-capped San Bernardino Mountains in the distance. Here at the tip of Point Loma, the statue and the nearby **Old Point Loma Lighthouse** provide two historic focal points for visitors to the Cabrillo National Monument. At the other end of this windswept 144-acre park, Sunset Cliffs Park affords exactly the sort of early evening spectacle its name suggests. Ironically, Cabrillo never lived to report his discovery to the king of Spain. He was injured in a fall and died after infection set in two months later on the same voyage of discovery.

Right: A dramatic statue pays tribute to Juan Rodriguez Cabrillo, the first European explorer to discover San Diego.

Below: Fort Rosecrans National Cemetery overlooks both sides of Point Loma, a short distance from its southerly tip.

Above: Downtown San Diego, with Coronado Island in the foreground, as seen by visitors to the statue of explorer Juan Rodriguez Cabrillo on Point Loma.

Left: A white picket fence and flowering shrubs complete a picture of the Old Point Loma Lighthouse as a quaint piece of antiquity.

From rocky vantage points in the Cabrillo National Monument, one can see California gray whales on their annual migratory journey from Alaska to Baja California. A sheltered viewing station and high-powered binoculars enhance the viewing experience for visitors in mid-January when as many as two hundred whales have been spotted on a clear day.

But for many visitors and especially picnickers, the chief attraction is the Old Point Loma Lighthouse. Situated on a scenic bluff overlooking its more modern replacement, the old lighthouse was turned over to the Park Service in 1931.

OLD TOWN

San Miguel was renamed San Diego in 1602 when Spanish colonialist **Sebastian Vizcaino** dropped anchor in the same bay that had so impressed Juan Cabrillo sixty years earlier. Vizcaino had been told not to rename earlier discoveries, but on November 12th, the day of the Feast of San Diego de Alcala, he made an exception and the name stuck. But this San Diego remained home to only a few settlements of Native Americans for another one-hundred and sixty-six years, until the arrival of an overland expedition of Franciscan monks from Mexico. Their leader, **Father Junipero Serra**, established California's first mission near the south bank of the San Diego River. A small colonial settlement sprang up nearby, and despite many skirmishes with the Native Americans of the area this settlement, known today as **Old Town**, was the birthplace of the city of San Diego.

The unofficial center of Old Town is a collection of shops and restaurants built in the design of colonial Mexico. The **Bazaar Del Mundo** overflows with flowering vines and the bright reds, purples, pinks and whites of the most effusive planters.

Clay-potted flowers and a tiled fountain add a gentle Mexican touch to Old Town, for diners and strollers alike.

An entrance to Old Town.

Baskets and barrels bearing goods for sale bring Old Town shoppers back to the 19th century.

The Bazaar Del Mundo is a center for shops and restaurants in Old Town.

Carrying the Old Town to even greater heights is Dodson's Corner, an oxymoronic modern, yet 19th-century shopping complex which includes curio shops, souvenir stores, restaurants and outdoor kiosks selling everything from turquoise jewelry to Indian blankets.

Old Town San Diego State Historic Park was officially named in 1968 and in spite of one hundred and one years of decay, including the fire of 1872, many of the original buildings were available for restoration at their original site about three miles away from the waterfront. Today, a walk through the area between Congress and Juan Streets is like stepping back into the youthful years of the first European settlement in California. The buildings have been renewed or rebuilt with tremendous attention to detail and historic accuracy. An old hacienda, horse stables and a chapel are among the many impressive restorations that make Old Town a life-size museum. The original Spanish colonial adobe buildings of the 1800s are a special attraction, their sun-bleached, whitewashed walls adding a bright air to an already irrepressibly cheery environment. Some of the more interesting old buildings are Las Casas de Estudillo, Machado y Stewart, the Seeley Stable and the store of Racine and Laramie, all of which have been restored and contain exhibits. Park staff and volunteers stroll the streets and lanes in period costume on Wednesdays and the first Saturday of the month, lending an extra touch of realism to an already festive atmosphere.

Visitors find that Old Town fairly overflows with lush greens and flowers at every turn.

Abundant palms and whitewashed walls evoke old San Diego in an Old Town church.

OLD TOWN TROLLEY

No self-respecting post-Civil War metropolis would be caught without an urban mass transit, and Old Town San Diego was no exception. The exception lies in the fact that more than a hundred years after the Old Town Trolley rumbled through the intersection of Mason St. and San Diego Ave. it is celebrating a revival of sorts. It no longer runs on the original 37 miles of track (rubber wheels are more versatile), and the drivers now double as tour guides, but the full two-hour narrated city tour is undoubtedly more comfortable and informative than the original. It has nine stops all within easy walking distance of almost every Old Town attraction, and numerous downtown sights including the

The Old Town Trolley provides an informative narrated tour of Old Town and a welcome break for weary walkers.

Embarcadero and the Gaslamp District. The Old Town Trolley also crosses over the Coronado Bridge for a panoramic view of San Diego Bay, the city skyline, Balboa Park and Coronado Island. With daytime departures every thirty minutes virtually all year round, the Old Town Trolley is an entertaining and informative trip back in time to 1888, when 37 miles of track and trolley cars provided the most technologically advanced means of getting around 19th-century San Diego.

PARKS IN OLD TOWN

The green hills of **Presidio Park** offer some of the earliest history of San Diego. It was here that Father Junipero Serra and a company of priests and soldiers set up the Mission San Diego de Alcala in 1769, claiming the area for the Queen of Spain. Five years later the site was designated a Royal Presidio - a fortress - and the mission was moved to a location about six miles to the East. Today, Presidio Park is a placid refuge for picnickers and recreationists. The **Junipero Serra Museum**, high atop a 160 foot hill, occupies the original site of the mission, housing artifacts from the period of the first European settlement of San Diego.

Also within the general area of Old Town is **Heritage Park**, the site of several grand Victorian homes, all relocated from other parts of San Diego and restored. The present day brightly colored mansions house restaurants, offices, stores and a bed-and-breakfast inn.

The Junipero Serra Museum looks down on Old Town from its hilltop position among the lawns and trees of Presidio Park.

Ornate and restored Victorian houses brighten the grass lawns of Heritage Park.

Entrance to Heritage Park, San Diego's restored Victorian Village.

The cracked white walls of the Mission San Diego de Alcala and its distinctive bell tower make a brilliant backdrop for the yellow blooms of a mission garden.

Dark wooden pews, a red tile floor and white walls identify the rustic interior of a sanctuary in the San Diego Mission.

SAN DIEGO MISSION

California's first mission, an outpost of colonial Spain, was originally built in 1769 atop a hill overlooking the future site of Old Town. But as imposing a location as it occupied, **Mission San Diego de Alcala** suffered for a lack of water, scarcity of food and testy relations between the resident soldiers and local Native Americans. Within five years the mission was moved downhill and upstream to a more practical site along the San Diego River. Unfortunately the new mission did not leave its problems behind. Efforts to convert the natives from tribal ritual to Catholicism met with disastrous results. In 1775 Natives attacked and burned the fledgling mission to the ground, murdering **Franciscan Padre Luis Jayme**. Fortunately the following hundred years proved much kinder to Mission San Diego Alcala and in 1976 Pope Paul VI gave it the honored title of minor basilica. Today, the mission's bleached-white adobe walls, stout belltower and arid courtyard provide a beautiful setting for an important religious monument. The mission museum, named for the martyr Padre Luis Jayme, contains artifacts from the dark days of its early history.

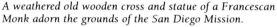

A weathered old wooden cross and statue of a Francescan Monk adorn the grounds of the San Diego Mission.

Ivy borders an exterior brick pathway of the Mission.

The Crucifixion spotlighted against an adobe wall of the Mission.

Downtown buildings catch the last minutes of sunlight as dusk descends on the waterfront.

Modern downtown architecture comes to life with lights, after dark.

DOWNTOWN

On April 15, 1867, three hundred and twenty three years after Juan Cabrillo's discovery, the steamer Pacific puffed into San Diego Bay carrying a man with a vision, intent on buying himself a town. **Alonzo Erastus Horton** arrived in a San Diego that consisted of a few crumbling adobes and a loose clutch of clapboard wooden buildings huddled in the hills some distance from the beach. The flat-lands down by the ocean seemed swampy and useless. So, when Horton bought up 960 acres of waterfront most locals considered it some kind of a joke and Horton some kind of a fool for paying an average of about twenty-seven cents an acre.

But five years later, when much of San Diego was destroyed in a fire, Alonzo Horton was ready with a plan for a new waterfront city. And, he just happened to own the land on which the city could be built. Merchants eager to rebuild their businesses bought a piece of Horton's dream and seemingly over night San Diego had become a port town with a future. The **Santa Fe Railroad** steamed into town in 1885, terminating the first transcontinental rail link two blocks from the water and sealing Alonzo Horton's place in history as the father of downtown San Diego.

Of course, Horton and his contemporaries wouldn't recognize the city today. The few flickering gas lamps of yesteryear have been overwhelmed by a shimmering sea of neon and incandescent lights which define San Diego's dynamic skyline. A concerted effort by politicians and business leaders in recent decades has revived the spirit of forward-looking development here. Drab and dated buildings have been torn down and replaced by elegant new hotels, upscale condominium complexes and trendy cafes, all of which have attracted newcomers and natives alike to a newly developed city center that has retained an open and outdoor character.

Mirrored glass office buildings and bank towers reflect the seemingly ubiquitous blue skies and sunshine throughout a downtown core where some of the grand old edifices of the past remain as grand and functional as ever.

The U.S. Grant Hotel is a perfect example. White-gloved doormen, a smooth marble lobby and sparkling chandeliers hearken back to a more gracious time in the years impressive Santa Fe Depot, built in 1915 on the site of the original train station.

Glowing green lights accentuate one of the more innovative works of architecture in downtown San Diego.

The Santa Fe Depot is a beautifully restored rail station that remains an impressive functioning landmark of San Diego.

The U.S. Grant Hotel is a distinguished senior citizen of downtown San Diego.

SAN DIEGO TROLLEY

The **San Diego Trolley** is much more than just a latter-day paean to the city's history. Indeed, streetcars clattered through some 37 miles of local streets more than a century ago, but today's trolley also serves as the keystone of a well-integrated transit system that connects air, seas and land travellers throughout virtually the entire San Diego region. For commuters, the Metro Transit System (MTS) is a vital link between their homes in far flung suburbs and their jobs in the downtown core. For leisure-seekers it is a congestion-free route to the theater, the park, a sporting event, the beach or

The San Diego Trolley runs throughout the city and south to the Mexican border.

the border. And for long-distance travellers it is a cheap and practical way to get to the airport or seaport.

Trolley lines extend to within 100 feet of Mexico and Tijuana, making for a scenic and exotic excursion at a bargain price. One way fares range from $1 to $3 depending on the route chosen and distance travelled, with special passes available for unlimited rides on all MTS buses and trolleys. This inexpensive

transportation link for those who would visit Mexico also works the other way, as an attractive option for Mexican artists who bring their works to San Diego, a ready market that easily embraces its Mexican and Spanish colonial cultural heritage.

The San Diego Trolley continues to chart new routes through major expansion projects that have begun to extend trolley service into Old Town, Mission valley and North County.

HORTON PLAZA

It's hard to conceive of a more appropriate name for **Horton Plaza**. After all, it was Alonzo Horton himself, who had the original dream of a vibrant new downtown core for San Diego back in 1867. Since then the downtown has evolved, but at no time has more life been pumped into downtown San Diego than with the development of Horton Plaza. The outdoor Plaza itself is a marvel of restored turn-of-the-century elegance as befitting of San Diego as Piccadilly Circus is to London. Occupying seven city blocks and firing a renaissance for all of the downtown area, the Horton Plaza retail complex's award-winning architecture provides an attractive yet practical home for a score of fine restaurants, several theaters, a deluxe hotel, four major department stores and more than a hundred assorted shops. Across Broadway stands the venerable **U.S. Grant Hotel**, subject of an $80-Million facelift, and a stately reminder of days past, when the neighborhood was known only as the **Gaslamp Quarter**, and Horton Plaza was still a figment of the future.

Jessop's Clock, set amidst the banners and walkways of the six-level Horton Plaza.

The fountain at Horton Plaza has become a landmark of the modern shopping and entertainment complex.

Apples and oranges flow from cornucopias into neat stacks at the farmer's market in Horton Plaza.

Shopping in Horton Plaza includes a stop at the Warner Bros. Studio store for film memorabilia.

Horton Plaza's modern architectural design is itself an eye-pleasing attraction.

An arching overhead sign welcomes traffic to the Gaslamp Quarter, the historic heart of San Diego.

THE GASLAMP QUARTER

Alonzo Horton's 19th century vision for San Diego included a dynamic financial center which quickly took shape on sixteen blocks of territory in the approximate area of Fifth Avenue, between Broadway and Market Street. It became known as **The Gaslamp Quarter** for its ubiquitous early street lights and Victorian commercial buildings. Alas, as San Diego outgrew its tiny economic heart, the Gaslamp Quarter fell into disrepair, evolving into a neighborhood of musky taverns and seedy dance halls. Alonzo Horton's New Town had developed a tawdry edge which remained until the mid-1970's when preservationists banded together, raised funding and began the task of reviving the neighborhood. Having seen both the best and worst of times, the heart of 19th century boomtown San Diego survived long enough to capture the city's imagination. Today The Gaslamp Quarter is a National Historic District with shops, galleries, theaters and restaurants. A walking tour reveals the Victorian roots of the area including some of the brick firewalls which saved much of the neighborhood from the great fire of 1872. A century after igniting the urban economy, the Gaslamp Quarter has re-entered the city scene as one of the hottest attractions of downtown San Diego.

A restored old horseless carriage rolls past a Victorian building in the Gaslamp Quarter.

The long piers of the Port of San Diego provide a functional interface between the shipping industry and the city.

THE HARBOR

The best of all perspectives from which to experience San Diego may well be from the water, for this is a city whose working and recreational life is tied inextricably to the Pacific Ocean. From naval operations to harbor cruises to the America's Cup races, the defining events of daily life very often take place in **San Diego Harbor**. Cruise ships sail for destinations near and far from the art deco cruise ship terminal at the foot of B Street. Harbor cruises and tours of the bay from the B Street and Broadway piers add to the happy seaborne traffic while yachts of wealth glide in and out of the world famous **San Diego Yacht Club**, in recent years the home of the America's Cup sailing races. By land, a most spectacular view of the proceedings would include a stroll along the **Embarcadero**, a seawalk studded with docks, restaurants and seagoing vessels of every description.

An old riverboat nestles comfortably beside more modern modes of transportation in and around San Diego Harbor.

MARITIME MUSEUM

A turn-of-the-century riverboat tied up at the foot of Ash Street doubles as the headquarters for the **San Diego Maritime Museum**. Fairly creaking with history, the Berkeley was based at San Francisco for over fifty years. The Berkeley carried thousands of refugees from the great San Francisco earthquake of 1906 to safe haven in Oakland. The Berkeley is part of a collection of three vessels that make up the Maritime Museum. The second is the restored 90-odd year old Scottish steam yacht Medea. The third, and by far the most famous, is the **Star of India**, a fully-restored and functioning windjammer. A fixture of San Diego harbor for some seven decades, the Star of India remains an important historic waterfront landmark.

The windjammer Star of India (foreground), for decades a San Diego landmark, joins the Berkeley as a dockside attraction of the waterfront.

Maritime memorabilia on display at the Maritime Museum of San Diego.

Opposite page:
A fully operational sailing vessel, the Star of India is also the main attraction of the Maritime Museum.

Opposite page, inset:
The massive wheel of the Star of India, one of San Diego's most enduring landmarks.

SEAPORT VILLAGE

The entrance to Seaport Village, a popular waterfront dining and shopping complex.

A water fountain makes for a cooling respite for pedestrians in Seaport Village.

In a city already famous for fine restaurants, entertainment and shopping with a hybrid southwestern-coastal identity, **Seaport Village** stands out as a unique experience. San Diego's maritime history is commemorated in style and with exquisite taste in this fourteen-acre waterfront shopping and dining complex. Here, the charm of New England merges with the warmth of the Spanish Mission, providing an attractive link between the waterfront, the convention center and harborside hotels. A boardwalk traces the shore for a quarter mile while cobblestone and dirt road paths wind between more than seventy-five restaurants and shops selling items from the quaint to the bizarre. A continuous happy explosion of futuristic electronic sound emanates from the hi-tech Sega family entertainment center while more nostalgic strains of organ lead children of all ages to the ornate, old-fashioned Broadway Flying Horses Carousel.

Right, above: The Broadway Flying Horses Carousel, an 1890 amusement park ride was restored and brought to Seaport Village from Massachusetts in 1980.

Right: The rustic Harbor House on an old dock is a popular restaurant in Seaport Village.

A tranquil pond and world-class landscaping are just two pleasing features of Seaport Village.

Lights reflected off the water set an inviting evening atmosphere.

The Hyatt Regency and Marriott resort hotels provide a modern backdrop for the stylish restaurants and shops of the waterfront.

CONVENTION CENTER

Positioned on the waterfront walkway next to the luxurious Marriott Hotel and Marina, the **San Diego Convention Center** is a subtly elegant, contemporary masterpiece of architecture. Designed by world-famous architect Arthur Erickson, this $160-million complex develops a maritime feel with a roof of billowing white sails, emerald green skylights, angled beams of concrete and sprawling open plazas leading down to the water. In addition to state-of-the-art convention facilities, half a dozen tennis courts along the roof's edge form a functional expression of the carefree side of San Diego's character.

Right: The nautical architectural style of the San Diego Convention Center can be felt indoors as well as out.

Below: The San Diego Convention Center strikes a distinctly nautical profile, a highlight of the waterfront.

BALBOA PARK

Arguably the finest urban park in all of America, San Diego's **Balboa Park** is a major center of culture, science, art, theater, music and sports, enveloped in a beautifully wrinkled cloak of lush green canyons, hills and gardens. And, as Alonzo Horton had a vision for the urban development of the city, a nursery owner named **Kate Sessions** had an inspiration that became Balboa Park. Twelve hundred acres of scrub land was originally set aside for park development in 1868. But, for some twenty years nobody seemed to know what do with it until Kate Sessions began quietly planting one-hundred new trees from all over the world there each year. Ten years and a thousand tree-plantings later, Kate Sessions' inspiration took root in city hall. The Park Improvement Committee was formed and Balboa Park's future was assured. Today the park includes some of the finest land-scaping, exotic gardens and fantastic architecture ever assembled in one place.

From the deep symbolism of the **Japanese Friendship Garden**, to the blooming water lilies of the **Lily Pond**, to the orchids and five hundred other varieties of tropical plants in the **Botanical Building** nursery, Balboa Park remains a testament to the quiet inspiration of Kate Sessions.

Left: The ornate 200-foot California Tower soars above the tiled dome of the Museum of Man.

Below: The lush green space of Balboa Park is impressive, even from the air.

Bird of Paradise, one of the many exotic orchids found at the zoo.

Southern California is one of the only places outside Australia where eucalyptus trees occur in nature, providing a steady diet of eucalyptus for the resident Koalas of the San Diego Zoo.

In September of 1916 a local doctor and his brother heard the roar of a lion as they drove past Balboa Park and the grounds of the **Panama-California Exposition**. The fair, which included a live-animal display was soon to close, prompting Dr. Harry Wegeforth to think out loud, "Wouldn't it be wonderful to have a zoo in San Diego?" And so began Dr. Wegeforth's twenty-five year obsession to build a zoo. Today, the **San Diego Zoo** is home to more than eight hundred species of rare and endangered animals. And, in an age of theme parks and thrill rides, with many zoos in decline, San Diego Zoo continues to reach new heights in informative entertainment and scientific research. The legacy of nurserywoman Kate Sessions also thrives

here in the form of sixty-five hundred varieties of exotic plants which provide stunning and constantly changing backdrops for some displays, and integral elements of others. Such is the enormity of this one-hundred acre park within a park that it might be easy to miss the bust of one Dr. Harry Wegeforth at the entrance to San Diego Zoo.

Top left: More than 6,500 varieties of plant life flourish in San Diego Zoo.

Top right: Exotic Africa comes to life in many of the 800 species of animals at the San Diego Zoo.

Above: The elephant pen is home to several pachyderms like this one.

MUSEUMS

The roar of the lion that moved a man to build a zoo came from among a group of buildings that were originally built to be torn down, but eventually became the heart of San Diego's museum district. The intricately designed **Spanish-Moorish** buildings of the Panama-California Exposition of 1915 were spared the wrecking ball and today form a nucleus of substance and style for Balboa Park's superlative collection of museums. The Spanish theme was carried through the addition of several new buildings for the 1935-36 California Pacific International Exposition. Today the plaza and promenade originally built for the 1915 fair have become Balboa Park's main pedestrian mall.

El Prado passes through a stellar community of museums covering areas of interest ranging from flora and fauna to trains, planes, automobiles, art and history.

An imposing facade of columns and sculptures aggrandizes the entrance to the San Diego Museum of Art in Balboa Park.

A multitude of arches lend a gothic charm to walkways of the Museum of Man.

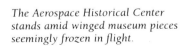

The Aerospace Historical Center stands amid winged museum pieces seemingly frozen in flight.

Among the grand architecture of the museums of Balboa Park one can find several excellent venues for theater and cinema. At one end of El Prado, across from the grand facade of the **Museum of Natural History** and the **Plaza de Balboa fountain** stands the **Reuben H. Fleet Space Theater and Science Center**. This marriage of theater and science cannot be undertaken in more spectacular fashion than in the world's largest omnimax theater and the Imax/Monimax films which are shown here every day. Also on El Prado, but at the opposite end of the museum district just beyond the **Museum of Man**, the **Simon Edison Center for the Performing Arts** houses three small, intimate theaters. Outdoor stages at the **Edison Center** provide an exquisite setting for evening performances of the lively arts.

The Casa del Prado Theater is one of the chief attractions of the museum district of Balboa Park.

An old street clock stands in a colorful garden near the Old Globe Theater of Balboa Park.

The Old Globe Theater, venue for Shakespearean plays, is located beside Balboa Park's Museum of Man.

If it was not recorded in the history it might be hard to believe that a nudist colony and a village of midgets were once located in Balboa Park. They were two of the more bizarre attractions of the 1935 Exposition. And while these dubious attractions have long since faded from memory, the fair did leave behind a legacy in the form of a number of small houses which have since become known as the **Spanish Village Arts and Crafts Center**. Situated between the Museum of Natural History and the Zoo, the center provides studios for local artisans to demonstrate their skills and sell arts, crafts and jewelry. Where spectators once filled bleachers to gawk at nudists and dwarves, park visitors now can board a miniature train for a half-mile ride, or ride the nearby antique carousel.

Clay pots and cacti combine for excellent effect outside a Spanish Village shop.

A huge archway provides a becoming entrance to the shops of the artisans of Spanish Village.

Original paintings, many painted in small studios on site, decorate the walkways and plazas of Spanish Village.

Potted plants and bright tiles highlight the entrance to a store in Balboa Park's Spanish Village.

The Lily Pond reflects the beauty of the Botanical Building in Balboa Park.

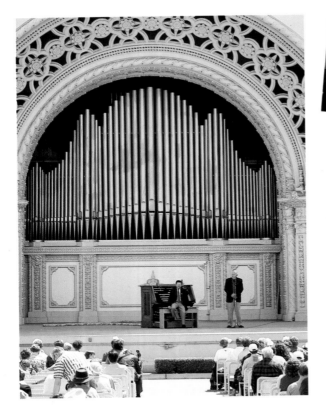

Water lilies abound in the
Lily Pond at the Botanical Building in Balboa Park.

The Spreckels Organ Pavilion in Balboa Park is the setting for some rare and unusual entertainment from the pipes of what may be the world's largest outdoor organ.

A long, thin island of flowers divides the roadway as it leads south from El Prado and around what may well be the largest outdoor pipe organ in the world. That distinction befits the big sound of the **Spreckels Organ** and its five thousand pipes, for this immense musical instrument forms the backbone of the Spreckels Organ Pavilion. Named for the millionaire who built a railroad connecting San Diego and Arizona, **John D. Spreckels**, the organ is played in free concerts every Sunday afternoon. Local military bands, gospel groups and barbershop quartets hold concerts here on summer evenings. And, each December, a massive Christmas tree and life-size nativity display draws throngs of winter visitors into Balboa Park.

Also popular with crowds in the Park is the Lily Pond, filled with giant koi fish and blooming water lilies. A popular spot with photographers, the waters of the pond reflect the latticed, open air nursery of the Botanical Building which houses a spectacular orchid collection. Musicians, mimes and jugglers perform on the lawns next to the Lily Pond in front of the Botanical Building.

AIRPORT

In 1925 ex-army pilot **T. Claude Ryan**, with a small fleet of biplanes he called Ryan Airlines, began shuttling passengers between San Diego and Los Angeles aboard the first regularly scheduled airline in the United States. A couple of years later a man nicknamed Slim, asked Ryan if he could build a plane capable of flying non-stop between New York and Paris. He wasn't certain it could be done, but Ryan went ahead anyway and built the **Spirit of St. Louis**, which **Charles Slim Lindbergh** flew on his history-making trans-atlantic flight. San Diego's airport was christened **Lindbergh Field** one year later and remains the city's center of aviation to this day.

Left: A commercial airliner departs from San Diego's Lindbergh Field airport.

Below: An aerial view of San Diego, with Lindbergh Field visible in the foreground (and Coronado Island in the background).

NAVY

The Navy arrived in San Diego in 1898 when the old iron gunboat USS Pinta clanked and wheezed her way into the harbor. More ships of war followed and by 1905 it became clear that more than anything else, this was a Navy town. That was the year that 60 men died in an explosion aboard the gunboat Bennington. The city mourned the deaths like a bereaved mother over the loss of an only son. And, three years later when the battleships of the **Great White Fleet** anchored offshore, jubilant residents built bonfires on the beach and rowed boats full of oranges out to the ships. The Navy had found a permanent place in the heart of San Diego.

San Diego is the strategic headquarters for the U.S. Navy's Pacific Fleet.

Navy vessels like this one are a predominant feature of marine activity in San Diego Bay.

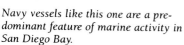

The U.S. Navy operates a major submarine base in San Diego on Point Loma.

The Naval yards of San Diego line the waterfront South of the downtown area.

SHELTER ISLAND AND HARBOR ISLAND

No matter how carefully he must have explored San Diego Bay back in 1542, Juan Cabrillo did not see **Shelter Island**. He would not have found it in 1942 either, because Shelter Island did not appear until 1950 when the port director decided to create it with the earth dredged up to deepen the shipping channel. Today those dredgings now support gigantic palms, resorts, restaurants and the world famous **San Diego Yacht Club**, in recent years home to the America's Cup, the most prestigious trophy in sailing yacht racing. Shelter Island and neighboring Harbor Island - the site of several hi-rise hotels and resorts - are actually not islands at all. Rather, these two long, narrow strips of real estate are attached to the mainland by short isthmuses which provide access for vehicles. Among the many notable restaurants on the two "islands" is one on **Harbor Island** which has a coast-guard-approved lighthouse tower, complete with blinking beacon.

Beautiful floral blooms make a garden-like milieu for the resorts and marinas of Shelter and Harbor Islands.

Bottom: Shelter Island is home to the San Diego Yacht Club and a myriad of boats.

Below: Harbor Island, a marine center for boats, restaurants and resorts, is situated between San Diego Bay and the airport at Lindbergh Field, which can be seen in the background.

CORONADO

In this city so beautifully and subtly influenced by old Spanish-style architecture it is surely ironic that possibly the most noticeable landmark is neither Spanish nor subtle. But, the San Diego-Coronado Bridge is arguably beautiful as an engineering marvel and for the sweeping views of the city it provides to all who cross it. This 2.2-mile long bridge crosses San Diego Bay to **Coronado Island**, named by the explorer Juan Rodriguez Cabrillo who first sighted "the crowned ones" in 1542. While San Diego began to develop its waterfront in the late 19th century, suburban Island residents built beautiful old Victorian-style homes, establishing for Coronado enough of an identity that it seceded from the rest of the city in 1891. But for the small Coronado ferry, there was no reliable connection between the island and downtown San Diego until the **San Diego-Coronado Bridge** was completed in 1969. A renewed passenger ferry service has since proven popular with commuters and others nostalgic for the days when Coronado was isolated from the mainland.

The San Diego-Coronado Island Bridge spans the Bay, joining the downtown area (right) with Coronado Island and the Municipal Golf Club (left).

From the air, the cyan waters of the Pacific Ocean seem a serene backdrop for the resorts, golf courses, and marinas of Coronado Island.

Beachgoers bask in the late afternoon sun on Coronado Beach.

The Coronado Bay Bridge lights up the waters of San Diego Bay.

The streets of Coronado Island exude a more laid-back atmosphere than their counterparts across the Bay in downtown San Diego.

The palm-lined fairways of Coronado Municipal Golf Club provide a tranquil contrast to the curving Coronado Bay.

Bicycles park in profusion near the Coronado Island landing of the Coronado Island-San Diego Ferry.

The Hotel del Coronado has been a movie set and a regular destination of celebrities from King Edward VIII and Wallis Simpson to Arthur Miller and Marilyn Monroe.

The "Del" is situated among the palms, beachside on one of the finest beaches on Coronado Island.

Built in 1888, the **Hotel del Coronado** has been California's premier ocean resort. Celebrities, royalty and heads of state have routinely graced this elegant wooden castle, with its red carpeted entrance, oak pillars and huge sparkling chandeliers. The Grand Ballroom overlooks the Del's priceless location on a smooth beach of white sand. The hotel has played host to 14 United States presidents since opening, and his Royal Highness, Edward, Prince of Wales, was a guest in 1920. The gourmet restaurant at the hotel is named in his honor. Today, the notched-pine walls fairly reverberate with more than a century of history amid the thousands of tourists who still come to the venerable Hotel del Coronado.

Nicknamed The Del, the hotel includes tennis among the numerous leisure activities for guests.

Circular red roofs and turrets set the Hotel del Coronado above and apart from its neighbors along the white beaches of Coronado Island.

OCEAN BEACH

Just north of Point Loma peninsula the rocky, sun-splashed cliffs give way to some of the most popular beaches of a city whose shores are considered its number one natural attraction. **Ocean Beach** is but the first of numerous world class beaches one would encounter on the north side of the city. Surfers, sunbathers, swimmers and volleyball players are as common as sunshine in the tiny community that sprang up years ago around Ocean Beach Pier. As one travels northward along the coast from here the beaches continue, sandy enclaves of sun and sea worshipers seemingly appearing around every curve in the road, from **Mission Bay** to **La Jolla** and beyond.

Ocean Beach Pier is a favorite meeting place for locals and visitors alike.

The diverse community of Ocean Beach is visible behind the famous Ocean Beach Pier.

MISSION BAY

A disappointing, swampy labyrinth of bays was all that Juan Rodriguez Cabrillo found in 1542 when he entered this place. He called it False Bay, but in the 1960's city planners decided to drain the swamp and create a 4,600 acre aquatic park. **Mission Bay**, with its labyrinth of waterways, islands, bay beaches sheltered from the power of the Pacific Ocean, and 17 miles of ocean side beaches is now easily one of the most popular recreation areas in all of San Diego. Where once there was marshland the visitor will find large expanses of manicured green space and a few resort hotels and attractions for tourists. Water skiers have a haven in Fiesta Island while power boats find their niche in the yacht pond and restaurants of Vacation Isle. A restored paddleboat, Bahia Belle completes any visit to Mission Bay with its spectacular daily sunset cruise.

The Bahia Belle, a genuine old paddlewheeler, plies the channels and waterways of Mission Bay to the delight of observers and passengers.

Left: Unlike the nearby ocean, the waters of Mission Bay provide an ideal surface for paddle boating.

Below: The manmade waterways of Mission Bay form a pleasant labyrinth for boaters.

SEA WORLD

Perhaps the biggest draw for visitors to Mission Bay is San Diego's world-famous **Sea World**. What once was simply a good aquarium has grown into a 100-acre marine theme park with enough to see and do and eat to leave even the most ambitious tourist happily exhausted. Take a glass tunnel through a frighteningly huge tank of sharks. Ride a moving sidewalk through a realistic Antarctic penguin colony. Watch a stage comedy in which a walrus plays straight-man for a seal. The highlight of any visit to Sea World is the killer whale show, a multimedia experience that includes music, video, audience participation, and above all, a stable of **Orcas** performing their water-gymnastics with a team of wet-suit clad trainers. A recent addition to this park is **Rocky Point Preserve**, where visitors are encouraged to feed and interact with bottlenose dolphins and observe Alaskan sea otters that were rescued and rehabilitated after the 1989 Exxon Valdez oil spill.

The killer whale pool is an azure jewel in the crown of Sea World San Diego, in the Mission Bay area.

Bottlenose dolphins seem genuinely amused by young visitors at Sea World's Rocky Point Preserve.

A pair of perfectly-synchronized Orcas jump for the joy of spectators.

The Shark Encounter gives visitors to Sea World an unparalleled view of the ocean's most frightening predators.

Mission and Pacific Beaches

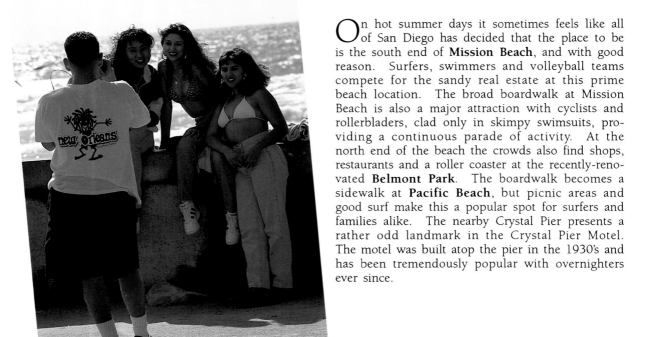

On hot summer days it sometimes feels like all of San Diego has decided that the place to be is the south end of **Mission Beach**, and with good reason. Surfers, swimmers and volleyball teams compete for the sandy real estate at this prime beach location. The broad boardwalk at Mission Beach is also a major attraction with cyclists and rollerbladers, clad only in skimpy swimsuits, providing a continuous parade of activity. At the north end of the beach the crowds also find shops, restaurants and a roller coaster at the recently-renovated **Belmont Park**. The boardwalk becomes a sidewalk at **Pacific Beach**, but picnic areas and good surf make this a popular spot for surfers and families alike. The nearby Crystal Pier presents a rather odd landmark in the Crystal Pier Motel. The motel was built atop the pier in the 1930's and has been tremendously popular with overnighters ever since.

Pacific Beach is famous for world-class surfing conditions.

Sunbathing at Mission Beach.

The boardwalk of Mission Beach is a continuous day time parade of activity.

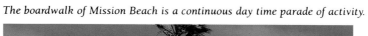

Biking at Mission Beach.

Crystal Pier extends far out into the surf at Pacific Beach.

Giant Dipper thrills passengers on a typically sunny and warm San Diego afternoon.

Belmont Park at night from the adrenalin-pumping top of the Giant Dipper.

Belmont Park seems virtually surrounded by beaches in this aerial view of the Mission Beach area.

LA JOLLA

Six thousand years ago a tribe of shell gatherers inhabited the beach area of **La Jolla**, leaving behind enough evidence for archeologists to trace their history as early residents of the San Diego area. Today, La Jolla is one of the most desirable suburbs of San Diego. Its curving coastline, green hillsides and elegant homes are reminiscent of Monte Carlo and the French Riviera. From the cross atop Mount Soledad the view is breathtaking. Point La Jolla, Ellen Browning Scripps Park and La Jolla Cove attract great attention for the raw beauty of the natural coast, while tall palms form a long line along Coast Boulevard providing the framework for neighborhoods of quaint shops and tiny restaurants. Native Americans once called this place "La Hoya", meaning "the cave", an allusion to the unusual rock formations on the shore. Today many non-Spanish speaking visitors mis-pronounce La Jolla (correctly pronounced "la hoy-a") but, the Spaniards who changed the spelling cannot be faulted for giving it a name that means "the jewel" in English.

Hang-gliding from the Glider Port of Torrey Pines.

An aerial view of La Jolla confirms the co-existence of beautiful beaches, greenery and the best of suburban living.

Sea Lions draw a crowd to the beach at La Jolla.

From sun worship to Sunday worship, La Jolla provides a setting of unparalleled aesthetic beauty. The striking post-modern spires of the Mormon Temple inspire the awe of all who come to church in the Golden Triangle district, while the violent clash of rocks and surf attracts congregations of man and animal to the beach. La Jolla Cove is a choice place to see both sea lions and harbor seals at different times of the year, and the best place to get close enough to detect the small "ear flaps" that distinguish sea lion from seal.

Like a kind of ice castle in an oasis, the Mormon Temple stands in stark contrast against the Golden Triangle district of La Jolla.

NORTH COUNTY

The 1930's were a time of depression, but ironically also an important period in the development of San Diego's **North County** region. The legendary crooner, Bing Crosby lived in Rancho Santa Fe at the time and while the rest of the country languished in hard times, he and some friends decided to build a race track where "the turf meets the surf" in the beach town of **Del Mar**. Today, the annual meeting of the Del Mar Thoroughbred Club is a major summer event in horse racing and a key fixture of Del Mar Fairgrounds.

Rancho Santa Fe was also a beneficiary of Bing Crosby's fame, with the Rancho Santa Fe Golf Course being the original home of the distinguished Bing Crosby Pro-Am. The area even then, was known mostly as cattle country, until the military took over most of 133,440 acre Rancho Santa Margarita just north of Oceanside. The result was Camp Pendleton and the transformation of once-sleepy Oceanside into a lively four-square center for the US Marines.

In the heart of cattle country, Rancho Santa Fe is now prime real estate and the location for many lavish mansions.

Brilliantly colored hot-air balloons against a deep blue sky are a breathtaking sight in Del Mar, where ballooning has become popular in recent years.

One of the largest in the San Diego area, the pier at Oceanside extends well beyond the surf.

A constant rainbow of color, the flower fields of Carlsbad are a beautiful distraction for motorists and aviators alike.

An aerial view of the Del Mar thoroughbred race track, home of the annual summer meet of the Del Mar Thoroughbred Racing Club.

WILD ANIMAL PARK

Some fifty miles north of the San Diego Zoo more than 2,500 animals from all over the world roam, virtual free citizens of an 1,800 acre savannah. **San Diego Wild Animal Park** is a cageless zoo that boasts a twenty-five year history of success with rare animals and tourists alike. Among the first inhabitants were twenty rare white African rhinos that had never been reproduced well in captivity. Within ten years, forty-two had been born in the Park. More recent successes include the first successful breeding of California Condors, which were extinct in the wild when the Park began reintroducing them. Visitors to the San Diego Wild Animal Park can ride a monorail through arid hills and see herds of zebra or impala, or even a giraffe family in a virtually natural environment. The Park is situated near **Escondido**, the center for a thriving region of freshwater lakes, farms, missions and wineries.

Boardwalks and bridges provide easy access through miles of trails in San Diego Wild Animal Park.

A rhinoceros mother and her baby depart a waterhole in the San Diego Wild Animal Park's impressive savannah environment.

San Diego Wild Animal Park, a zoo without cages, encourages visitors to interact with many of the birds and animals on display.

SOUTH BAY

Just one hundred feet beyond the last stop on a forty-five minute trolley ride from downtown is the frontier of the land from which San Diego draws so much of its culture, heritage and history. Indeed, San Diego was a Spanish settlement and a Mexican pueblo for years before a successful American campaign led California into the United States in 1850. Today, the international boundary border crossing between **San Ysidro** and **Tijuana** is one of the busiest in the world, averaging more than 100,000 crossings per day. Leaving the San Diego area here, it seems so appropriate that one of the last sights is a beach. Retracing one's steps from here would lead from Border Field State Beach and South Beach, to Imperial Beach, site of the world's longest running annual sand castle-building contest, and on up to the famous beaches of Coronado Island. The Interstate 5 route back to the city passes through Chula Vista, near the salt marshes of the Chula Vista Nature Interpretive Center, a wetland preserve for marine and animal life.

On the other side of the Mexican border, San Diego's southern neighbor is Tijuana, Mexico.

The Qualcomm Stadium is home to the San Diego Chargers football team and the San Diego Padres baseball team.

About ten thousand years ago, prehistoric "Del Mar Man" left his footprints on the beaches of San Diego. His presence as the earliest known visitor was confirmed in bones recovered in an archeological dig. There is no record of what Del Mar Man thought of all he surveyed, but it is fair to assume that like the Native Americans, the 16th century Spanish conquistadors, the Franciscan monks of the 18th century, and the land speculators and gold prospectors of the 19th century, Del Mar Man came here because he liked the warm climate and cool sea breezes of his surroundings. Like those who followed, he saw promise in **San Diego**. It was a promise that evolved from tentative beginnings into a reality that today is the envy of tourists and the pride of those who call this city home.

CONTENTS

Written by
Forbes Phillips

Edited by
Mia Forbes

Photographed by
Stefan Schulhof

James Blank   Cover

Bob Couey   51a
Ken Bohn   51b, 51c
Copyright © 1995 Sea World of California, Inc.
All rights reserved. Reproduced by permission.

Belmont Park   55a, 55b

Rick Geissler   62a
San Diego Chargers (NFL)

(Also available in French, German, Spanish, Italian and Japanese)